AF126969

Laboo's Space Trip

From **Mercury** to Pluto

Jasper Starfield

Hi, kids! What's up?

I'm Professor Laboo!

And, oh boy, do I have an adventure for you!

Today, we're going to space,

Swift, quick and fast.

We're going to see all the planets,

From the first one to the last!

First, I put on my astronaut suit,
And my helmet as well.

Then my space jetpack,
And I wave the Earth farewell!

"Hi, Moon! See you around!"
I wave as the Moon has her morning tea.

"Have fun, Laboo!" She says,
"Say hi to the planets for me!"

Pluto

All the planets

Go around the Sun,

Spinning and flying,

They have so much fun!

Saturn

Neptune

Uranus

Venus

Mars

Sun

Mercury

Earth

Jupiter

There it is! Our first happy planet!

"How are you today, Pretty Mercury?"
"I'm great as always," she tells me.
"Tiny, rocky, and quick as can be!"

Now we're off to the hottest place around,
Let's say hi to Venus together.
"Hi, Venus, have you cooled off?"
"How is the weather?"

"What can I do, Laboo!
I huff and I puff,
But for me,
There's no pool big enough!"

Now this next one you'll know well,
The Earth is my home, and yours too!
So, let's wave down to our friends,
Trees, oceans and animals at the zoo.

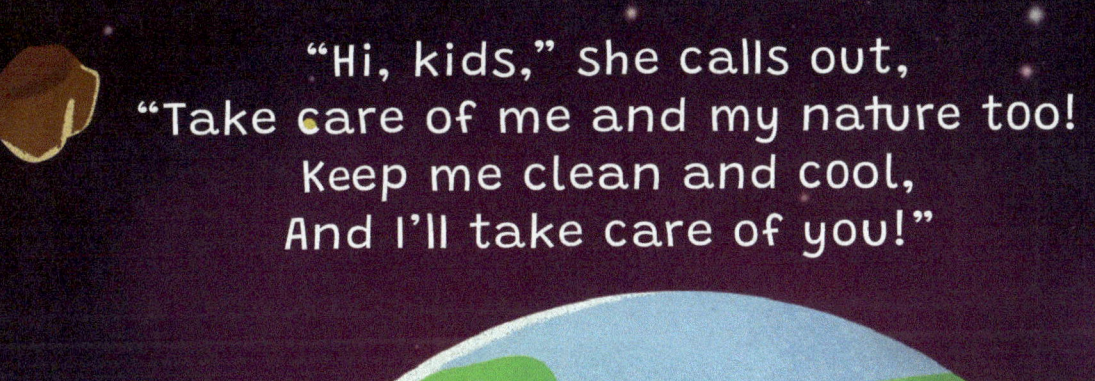

"Hi, kids," she calls out,
"Take care of me and my nature too!
Keep me clean and cool,
And I'll take care of you!"

Next is our tiny neighbor,
"Hi, how are you doing, Mars?"

"Great! I'm still glowing red,
Here among the planets and stars."

"Can you please,
Thank the people at NASA for me,

For the rover friends,
They sent to buzz around with glee?"

Now this one is special,
We can see it from so, so far.
That's because,
It's the biggest planet orbiting our star.

"I love your dress, Jupiter,
Your colorful swirls are sooo you!"
"That's why I'm the artistic one,
Thank you so much, Laboo!"

Now, kids, here is my favorite one,
Let's look at Saturn's beautiful rings.
"That's right, Professor Laboo,
I'm the only planet with wings."

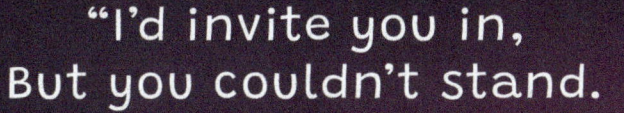

"I'd invite you in,
But you couldn't stand.

You'd just fall through me.
My gases are like quicksand!"

Look, kids, there's Uranus,
She's so bright and sleek.

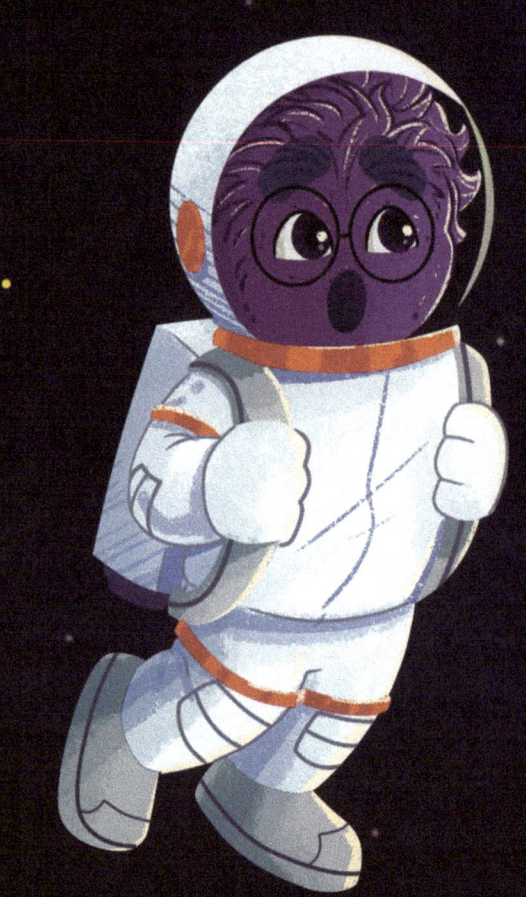

"And I spin the opposite way,
So I'm also quite unique!"

Now we're going far, Far away from the Sun.
Neptune is so cold, But still having fun.

"Hi, Laboo! That's right!
I like to be cozy and snug.
Curled up with my blankie,
And warm tea in my mug.

There's our last planet,
Let's see what he has to say.
"Hi, tiny Pluto,
How are you doing today?"

"I'm the last one,
And the smallest one too.
Why they say I'm not a planet,
I have no clue, Professor Laboo!"

Now it's time,
That our space adventure ends,
So, bye, Pluto!
Goodbye all my planet friends!

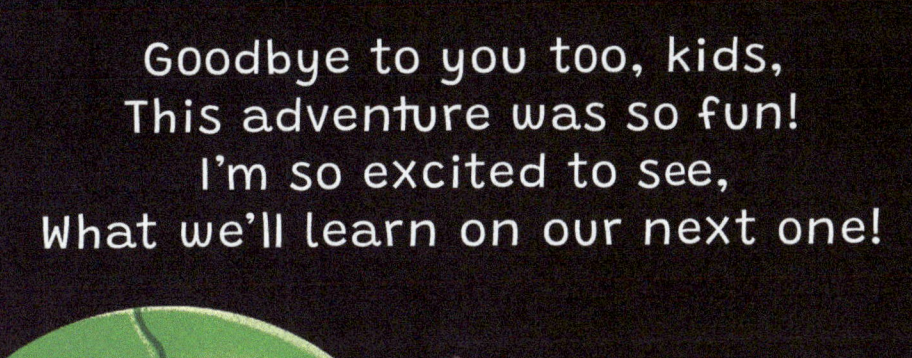

Goodbye to you too, kids,
This adventure was so fun!
I'm so excited to see,
What we'll learn on our next one!

www.ingramcontent.com/pod-product-compliance
Lightning Source LLC
LaVergne TN
LVHW070121100526
838202LV00011B/331